D1243884

Stars

Andres Llamas Ruiz
Illustrations by Ali Garoussi

Sterling Publishing Co., Inc.
New York

Illustrations by Ali Garoussi
Text by Andres Llamas Ruiz
Translated by Natalia Tizón

Library of Congress Cataloging-in-Publication Data

Llamas Ruiz, Andrés.
  [Estrellas. English]
  Stars / Andres Llamas Ruiz.
      p.   cm. — (Sequences of earth & space)
  Includes index.
  Summary: An illustrated description of the origin, evolution, and
activities of the stars, including the sun.
  ISBN 0-8069-9337-5
  1. Stars—Juvenile literature. [1. Stars. 2. Sun.] I. Title.
II. Series: Llamas Ruiz, Andrés.   Secuencias de la tierra y el
espacio.   English.
QB801.7.L5713   1996
523.8—dc20   96–9196
                                                           CIP
                                                            AC

1   3   5   7   9   10   8   6   4   2

Published by Sterling Publishing Company, Inc.
387 Park Avenue South, New York, N.Y. 10016
Originally published in Spain by Ediciones Estes
©1996 by Ediciones Estes, S.A. ©1996 by Ediciones Lema, S.L.
English version and translation © 1996 by Sterling Publishing Company, Inc.
Distributed in Canada by Sterling Publishing
% Canadian Manda Group, One Atlantic Avenue, Suite 105
Toronto, Ontario, Canada M6K 3E7
Distributed in Great Britain and Europe by Cassell PLC
Wellington House, 125 Strand, London WC2R 0BB, England
Distributed in Australia by Capricorn Link (Australia) Pty Ltd.
P.O. Box 6651, Baulkham Hills, Business Centre, NSW 2153, Australia
Printed and Bound in Spain
All rights reserved

Sterling ISBN 0-8069-9337-5

Table of Contents

The Origin of the Universe: the Big Bang

Do you ever wonder how the universe was formed? Scientists have posed that very question for a long time. Today, they believe that it was formed about 15 billion years ago by a great explosion known as the Big Bang.

Before the explosion, all the matter and energy of the universe had gathered and concentrated itself into a very small volume where temperatures reached millions of degrees. Then came a terrible explosion. At that moment, the universe began to expand in all directions.

Even though it may seem surprising, all we can actually see of the universe are the remains of that long-ago explosion.

As time goes by, the universe becomes larger as galaxies separate from one another at high speed. To explain this phenomenon, scientists came up with the Great Explosion, or Big Bang, theory.

1. All the matter and energy of the universe was originally gathered and condensed into a very small volume.

2. The temperature was very high

Scientists do not know what will happen as the universe continues to develop. Will it keep on expanding or will it contract, causing a new Big Bang?

Some stars take longer to form than others. Our own sun began to form "only" 5 billion years ago.

4

5

6

(more than 1.8 million degrees Fahrenheit or 1 million degrees centigrade).

3. Suddenly, there was an enormous explosion.

4. Giant hydrogen and helium gas clouds were formed.

5. These clouds separated into masses from which galaxies were created.

6. Billions of stars gradually appeared within these galaxies.

Giant Nebulae

Stars are formed inside immense interstellar clouds of gas and dust, called nebulae, which possess gravity and rotational movement. In time, gravity causes them to contract, and their speed of rotation increases.

When the cloud starts to contract, the matter inside condenses and heats up, causing a spectacular rise in temperature. This, in turn, begins a series of reactions that ulti-mately creates the stars. If the mass was very great at the beginning, it will create a warm star of either blue or white light. However, if the mass was not so significant, it will create a cooler star of either yellow or red light.

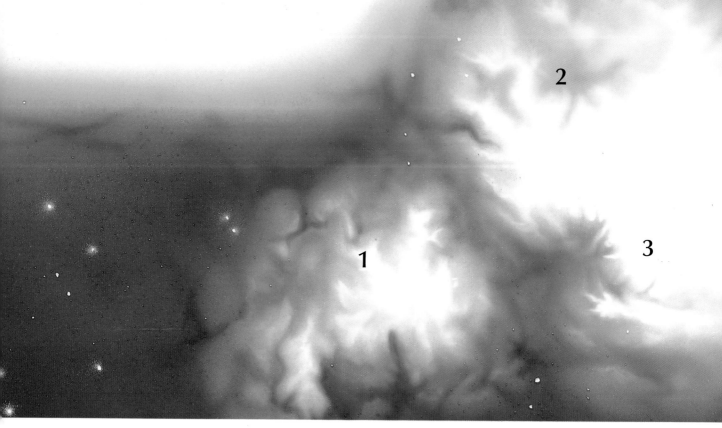

The masses of matter that travel in space, forming clouds of gas and dust, are very mysterious. They are very important since stars are formed from these clouds. One of these clouds is the Orion Nebula.

1. Cosmic clouds are important because they are the prime matter from which stars are born.

Density inside the cloud is very low. There is only one atom per cubic centimeter.

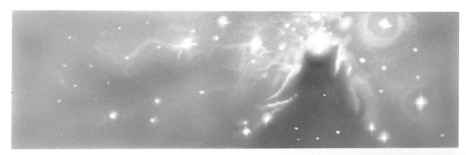

Nebulae have very different shapes. Here, you can see the Lyra Nebulae (a) and the Horsehead Nebula (b).

a

b

4

2. A nebula is formed primarily of hydrogen.

3. As the cloud rotates, gravity gathers particles, which form a mass that continues to grow.

4. As the mass grows, its internal temperature increases.

A Protostar Is Born

The making of a star is not a simple matter. A cloud of gas takes millions of years to contract. During this time, the nebula grows hotter—especially at the center. When the gas cloud (or part of it) contracts enough to become an independent sphere of warm gases, it is called a protostar.

Once a protostar is formed, it remains stable for several million years. Since gravity pulls the elements of a mass together, matter travels toward the protostar's center, which releases energy as heat. Thus, the temperature at the center of the protostar increases.

1

A gas cloud can contract into one or several concentrated nodules, each forming a protostar. Protostars are gigantic—much bigger than the entire solar system—and their temperatures are relatively low.

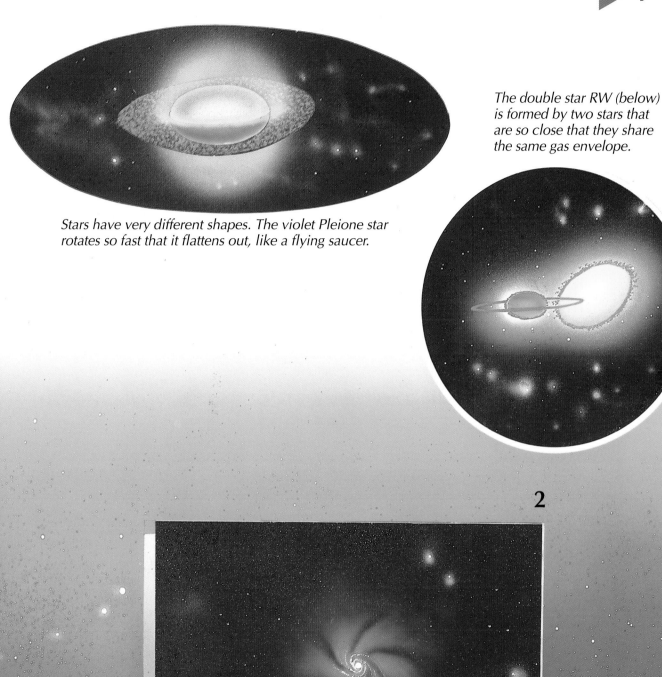

Stars have very different shapes. The violet Pleione star rotates so fast that it flattens out, like a flying saucer.

The double star RW (below) is formed by two stars that are so close that they share the same gas envelope.

2

1. Cloud matter gradually contracts toward the center. At this time, energy is released as heat.

2. The temperature at the protostar's center increases when gravitational energy becomes internal energy.

The rest of the contraction phase lasts tens or hundreds of millions of years.

A Star Is Formed

When the temperature at the cloud's center reaches many millions of degrees centigrade, hydrogen nuclei within the cloud begin to collide with one another until they form complex helium nuclei. This process is called nuclear fusion (a nuclear reaction), and huge amounts of energy are released, mostly as heat.

Then, the center of the cloud starts to "burn," and a star is born. After the new star has formed, energy produced by nuclear fusion causes it to swell like a balloon. As long as this energy is balanced by gravity, the star will remain stable, because, just as fusion causes the star to expand, gravitational energy tries to compress it. The stability can last for millions of years.

Protostars remain relatively stable for millions of years. At times, however, they suffer abrupt contractions, which increase the protostar's internal temperature and cause nuclear reactions (which will provide energy for the new star). The protostar then reduces to the size of a normal star.

Sometimes, several stars instead of just one are formed inside a cloud of gas.

Today, scientists believe that at least half the stars are "multiple," such as these that illuminate the gases of the Rosette Nebula.

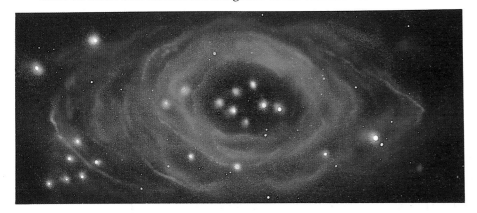

When a cloud of gas contracts, thousands of stars are born. These stars form groups. Very rarely is a star born far away from the influence of other new stars.

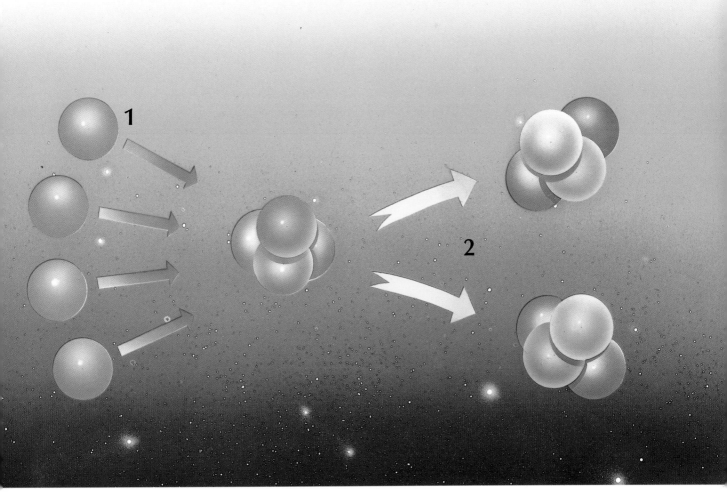

1. Stars are formed mainly from hydrogen, which is the simplest element.

2. Tiny hydrogen nuclei collide violently with one another and gather to form helium.

"Normal" Stars

Even if all stars look like similarly sized points of light, they are very different from each other. Some look like our sun, while others are much smaller, bigger, cooler, or warmer. The mass of some stars is only one-tenth the mass of the sun; other stars have thirty times the mass of the sun.

All stars have their own light—blue, yellow, or red in color. This is because each star has a surface temperature that influences the color of the light it gives off. The surface temperature of the sun, which gives off a yellow light, is 9,932°F (5,500°C). The temperatures of white stars range from 10,832°F to 18,032°F (6,000°C to 10,000°C), while red stars are the coolest at 5,432°F (3,000°C). Blue stars are the hottest of all, with temperatures that can reach 45,032°F (25,000°C).

Not all stars live the same length of time. Big stars have more hydrogen and their cores reach much higher temperatures than do those of small stars. This is why big stars "burn" hydrogen faster than smaller ones.

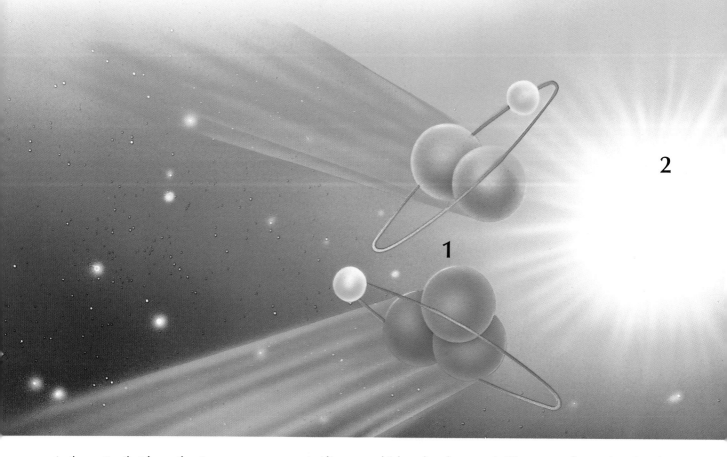

As the matter that forms the stars becomes more concentrated, hydrogen atoms collide with each other. This forms helium and releases large amounts of energy, which makes the stars shine.

1. The center of a star is so hot that there is a fusion between two colliding hydrogen nuclei.

Part of the Orion constellation, the star Rigel is 52,000 times brighter than the sun. Huge, brightly shining stars such as this one consume hydrogen so fast that they only shine for about a million years.

A star can have light of different colors:
Yellow star
Red star
Blue star
White star

2. This produces a release of energy as powerful as an atomic explosion!

3. As a result of the union, helium is formed. The energy produced then comes to the surface of the star in the form of light and heat.

4. As time passes, the star's hydrogen will be consumed and transformed into helium.

Our Star, the Sun

Is the sun a special star?

No. Our sun is simply one among the billion or so stars in our galaxy, although it is a very "special" star for us. It is so close (only 93 million miles or 150 million km) that it warms us and gives us light, which keeps life on earth.

The sun is a huge ball of gas, 861,800 miles (1,390,000 km) in diameter—108 times bigger than the earth's diameter. The center of the sun reaches a temperature of 50 million degrees F (10 million degrees C). As you already know, this is because there are nuclear reactions inside, where hydrogen turns into helium, releasing energy into space in the form of light and heat.

The solar corona, or crown, formed by electrons and "dust," is so huge that its diameter is twenty times larger than the sun's. If you want to see the crown, you will have to wait for an eclipse.

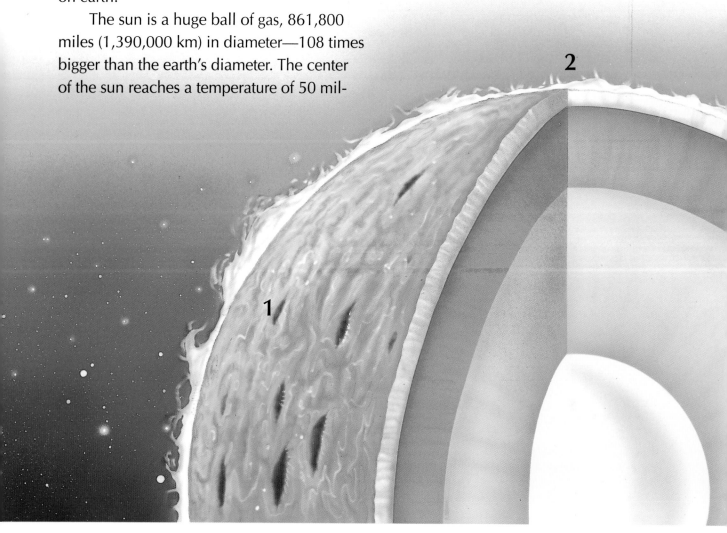

The gases that make up the sun are not evenly distributed. Scientists have discovered that the different layers that form the sun have very different characteristics, such as extreme temperature differences.

1. Solar spots are a little cooler than other parts of the sun. That is why they appear darker.

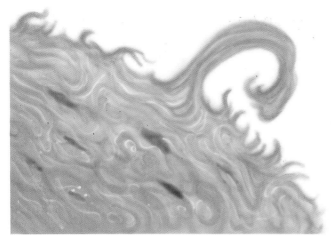

When the moon moves directly in front of the sun, there is a solar eclipse. The moon covers the entire solar disk; that is when you can clearly see the solar crown.

Formed by cooler gases, protrusions stick out from the sun's surface and erupt through the corona. They can form spirals that reach thousands of miles above the surface of the sun.

When solar winds hit the earth's atmosphere—particularly close to the polar regions—they produce col- *ored lights. The northern lights are called the Aurora Borealis; the southern lights are the Aurora Australis.*

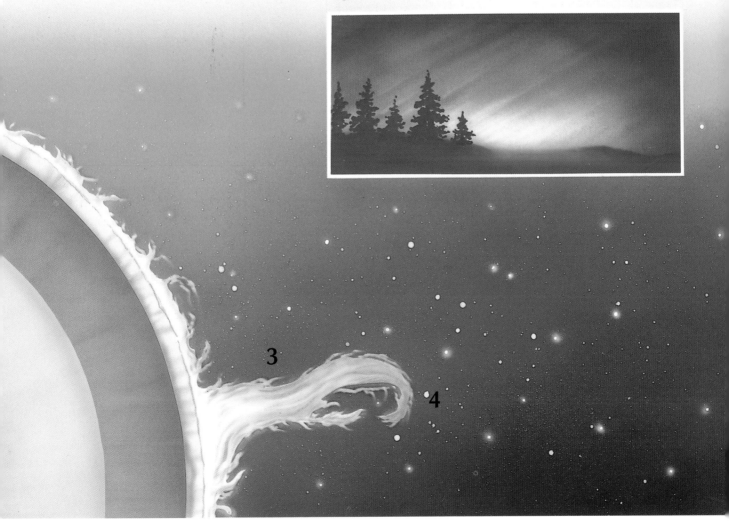

2. The temperature of the sun's surface (called the photosphere) is 19,472°F (6,000°C).

3. The chromosphere surrounds the sun's surface. It is very active and has many protrusions.

4. Solar activity sends particles in all directions, creating a "solar wind."

The Evolution of the Sun

Our sun is a yellow star. It appeared a little less than 5 billion years ago and will continue to live for another 5 billion more.

How was the sun formed? The same way that many other stars were formed. At first, there was a rotating cloud of gas made up mostly of hydrogen. Due to the speeding up of its rotational movement, the cloud flattened into a disk and part of the matter came together in the center to form a brightly shining sun. Then, the external layers of the cloud also contracted and solidified to form the planets of our solar system.

What will happen to the sun? All stars—even yellow ones like the sun—expand when they run out of combustible matter and became red giant stars. When this happens to our sun, life on earth will disappear.

In 5 billion years, the sun will become a red giant star. As a result, the amount of heat reaching earth will greatly increase, making life impossible.

1. The cloud of dust and gases contracts toward the center.

2. When it contracts, the center becomes warmer.

3. The external zone flattens like a disk.

Jupiter is the largest planet in the solar system. It is formed of gases—especially hydrogen and helium. In order for it to become a star, its mass would have to be sixty times greater than it is.

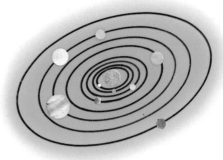

The sun and solar system move slowly in a circular orbit in our galaxy, taking 240 million years to complete a single revolution. What a trip!

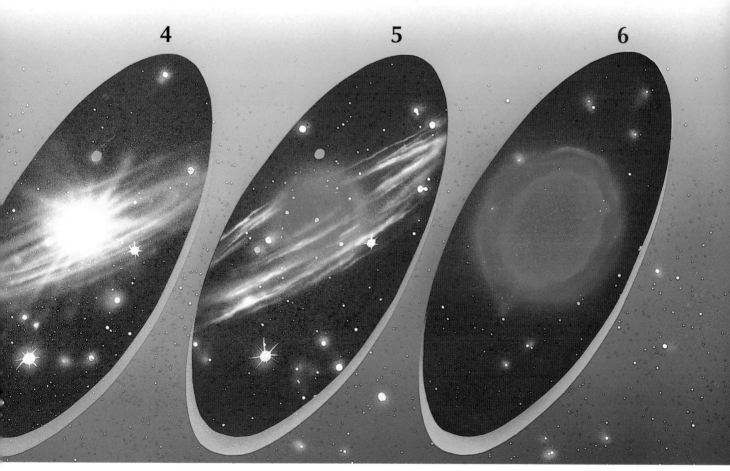

4. The center lights up with a bright flame. This is the birth of the sun.

5. In 5 billion years, the sun will become a red giant star.

6. As it expands, it will destroy all the planets closest to it, including the earth.

Red Giant

You have already seen that stars change over time. While the star is stable, shining uniformly, it is in its "main sequence" phase. Our sun is currently in this phase.

As a star continues to shine, its core builds up heat over the course of millions of years. During this time, hydrogen is consumed and helium condenses. At a certain point, the temperature at the center becomes so great that helium atoms form other, more complex atoms, such as carbon, oxygen, and iron.

As the heat of the star's core increases, its external layers expand and the star increases in size. When the star expands, its most external layers cool down and shine with a red light. This is why they are called red giant stars.

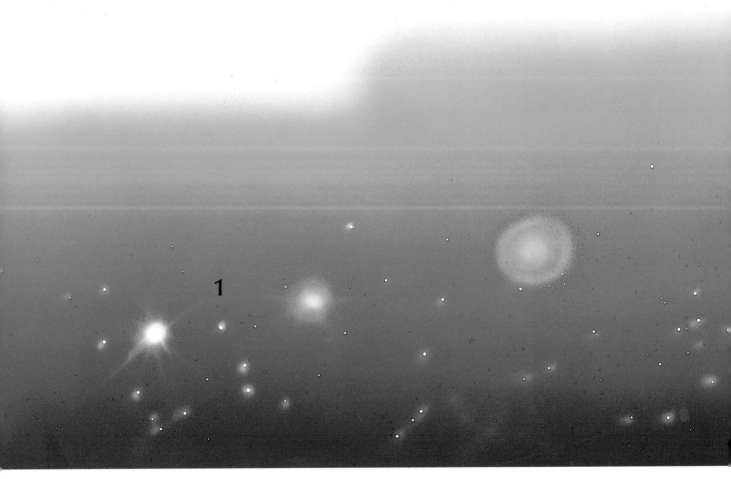

1

After shining for millions of years, all stars exhaust their internal combustible matter. Then, if a star heats up a lot more, it will increase in size. As a result, the external layers cool down and turn red. The result is a "red giant" star.

All stars become red giants when they run out of hydrogen. The largest ones become red "supergiants" like Betelgeuse, which has a diameter eight hundred times greater than that of the sun.

The largest known star is the Goat, a star in the Chariot. If it occupied the same position as the sun, its mass would reach all the way to Saturn.

Some stars have a diameter similar to the earth's even if their mass is similar to that of the sun. These stars are called white dwarfs; their density equals approximately one ton per cubic centimeter!

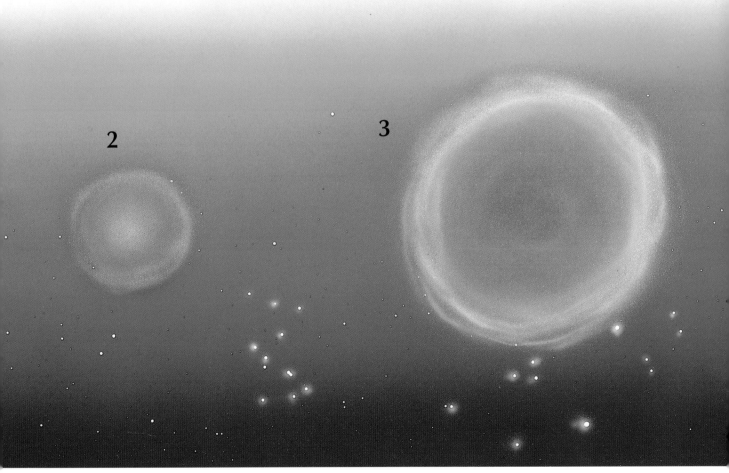

1. The star consumes its internal hydrogen.

2. When the internal temperature increases, the star expands.

3. External layers cool down and the star releases a red light. A red giant has formed; its diameter may be one hundred times larger than the sun's.

Supernovas

A red giant star does not last forever.

If a star continues to shine, its core will eventually run out of energy because the fusion process will stop when iron atoms and other heavy elements in the nucleus reach a certain proportion inside the star.

From that instant on, the core will begin to cool down and the star will not be able to produce enough heat to balance the strength of gravity. The star will then collapse into itself, causing the external cold and red layers to warm up. If the star is large enough, these layers will explode violently, producing a supernova. Since the external layers are the ones that explode, the larger the star, the greater the explosion. For some time, this explosion will shine in the sky like a galaxy!

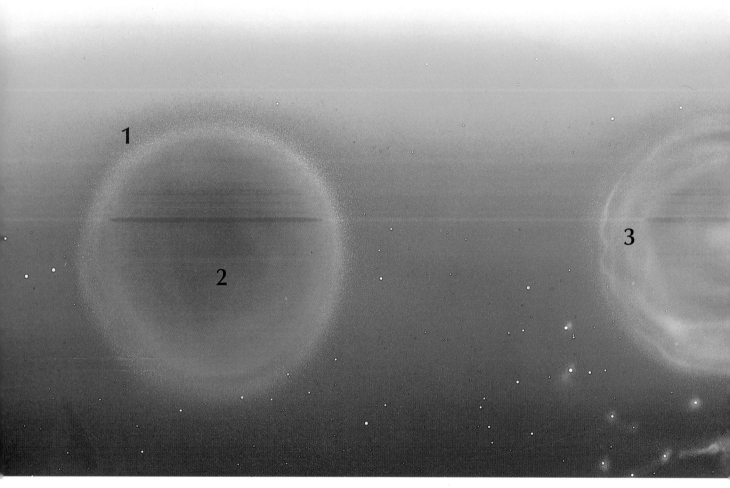

If the star is large enough, a supernova will appear after the explosion and can shine as brightly as a galaxy.

1. After shining for millions of years, iron atoms and other heavy elements formed in the core reach a certain proportion.

2. The fusion process stops and from that moment on, the core begins to cool down.

Ancient astronomers observed the explosion of a supernova in the year 1054. This explosion originated from what we know as the Crab Nebula, which continues to expand at a speed of 0.69 miles (1.1 km) per second.

You can see here the Cygnus Nebula, which is the remains of a supernova.

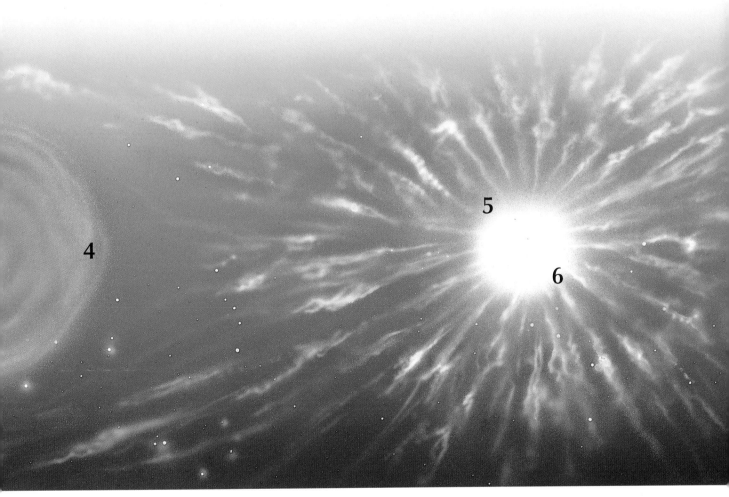

3. The star does not produce enough heat to balance the strength of gravity and the star collapses into itself.

4. The exterior layer heats up.

5. The star explodes.

6. It becomes a supernova, scattering its matter throughout space.

White Dwarfs and Neutron Stars

What happens after the explosion?

Part of the star matter then scatters into space. The remains can contract to form a neutron star or a black hole.

If the star that explodes is similar in size to the sun, its own gravity compresses it back to the size of a small planet, like the earth. At this point, the star has become a small white body, which we call a white dwarf.

On the other hand, if the star is larger than the sun, gravity creates a greater compression, forming a dense mass of neutrons. The entire mass of a star will be condensed to the size of a sphere 9.3 to 12.4 miles (15 to 20 km) in diameter. That mass is so concentrated that it can have a density of 100 million tons per cubic centimeter!

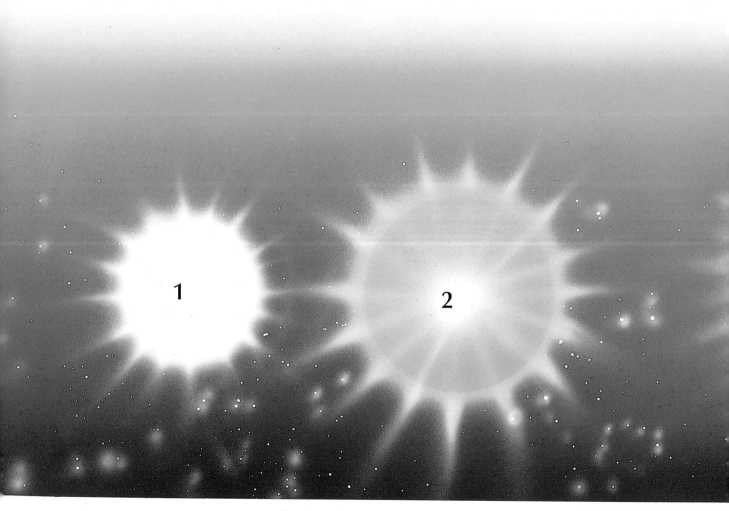

After the explosion phase, there is a small, very dense core where the star existed before. This core is a pulsar, or neutron star. It rotates at a very high and constant speed.

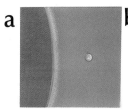   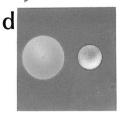

Ring nebulae are actually clouds of gas illuminated by white dwarf stars.

You can compare here the sizes of the following types of stars:
a. red giant - sun
b. sun - white dwarf
c. white dwarf - neutron star
d. neutron star - black hole

At the center of the Crab Nebula (below), there is a neutron star that rotates thirty-three times per second. With each turn, it sends electronic waves of energy and a flash of light. This is why this kind of star is called a pulsar. Pulsars are neutron stars that turn and send radio waves of electronic energy.

1. The hottest stars (blue and white) have a very fast development, lasting only 100 million years.

2. When they run out of hydrogen and helium, the stars turn into blue giants and then into red supergiants.

3 They can later explode in supernovas, which shine intensely for several months.

The Renewal of the Universe

Did you know that the death of some stars can help the birth of others?

You have already seen that when a supernova explodes most of its matter scatters into space. This matter contains complex atoms, such as carbon, oxygen, silicon, and iron. These elements become part of gigantic clouds of gas that will form new stars, although this time with more complex atoms.

Our sun is one of these stars. They are called second-generation stars, and they are formed from the matter of other stars. Scientists have discovered that only "gaseous" planets with hydrogen and helium atoms, like Jupiter, could be produced from the first stars. However, second-generation stars, like the sun, can form solid planets with rock and metals, like the earth!

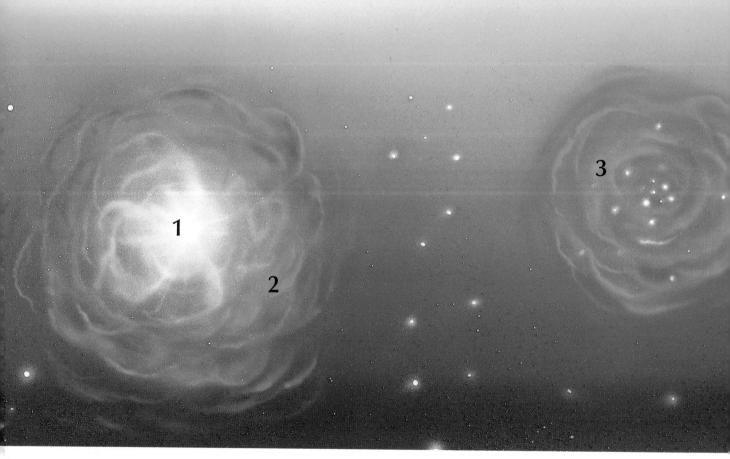

During the Big Bang, only the most simple atoms (hydrogen and helium) were formed, while during the supernovas the other atoms were formed.

This process is very important for us, since the sun was formed from a cloud of these more complex atoms.

1. The star explodes.

2. Matter disperses in all directions.

When the earth has disappeared completely, the sun will still exist as a red giant star for 2 billion years. Then the sun will explode and

turn into a white dwarf instead of a supernova. It will shine for millions of years until it gradually cools down and becomes a black giant star.

Neutron stars (below) can rotate more than six hundred times per second. Some neutron stars revolve around normal stars and, with their immense gravity, gradually attract the matter from other stars.

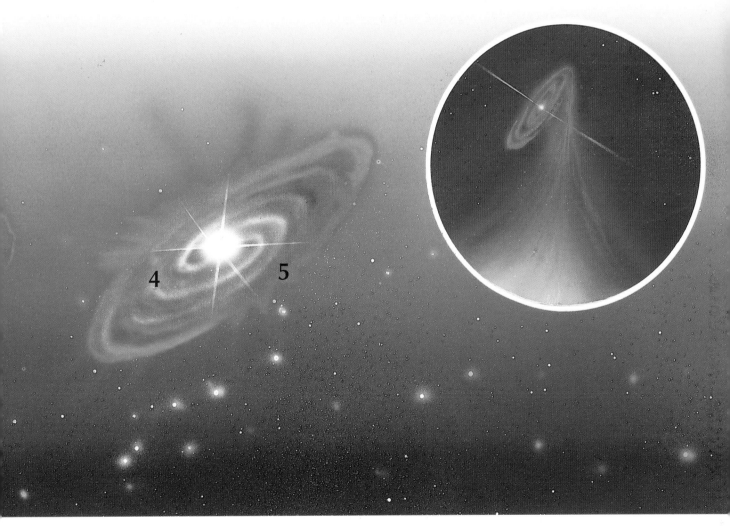

3. A gas nebula is formed in which there are more complex elements.

4. The stars that come from these nebulae contain complex elements that were created in old stars.

5. These complex elements allow for the formation of solid planets, like the earth.

Mysterious Black Holes

You have already seen that after the explosion of a supernova, part of its matter scatters into space, while the rest may create a neutron star or a black hole. Why is it a black hole?

As you already know, gravity is a force that attracts one object to another. It is very difficult to resist the attraction of gravity. For example, in space, only radio waves and light are likely to be capable of escaping from the attraction of a neutron star.

Black holes are smaller than a neutron star of the same mass, so their gravitational pull increases a great deal. In reality, their pull is so enormous that nothing that falls into their field of gravity can ever escape—not even light. That is why they are called black holes.

Today, we believe that there can be black holes at the nucleus of each galaxy.

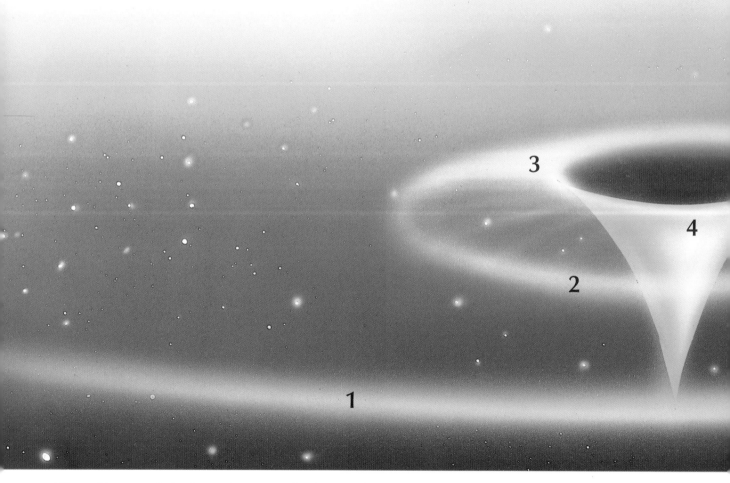

When a big star explodes, its remains compress greatly and can be concentrated into a very small space, forming a black hole. However, black holes do not last forever. The famous scientist Stephen Hawking has proven that black holes can, in time, evaporate very slowly and leave nothing behind.

1. After a star explodes, the leftover matter begins to concentrate.

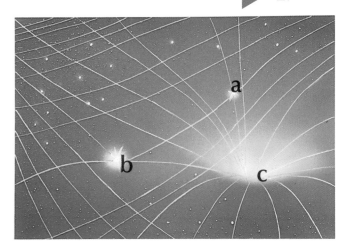

When a black hole is close to a star, it attracts parts of the star's matter. The attracted matter rotates in a spiral, sending X-rays that can be detected by astronomers. In reality, this is the only thing that we can "see" of a black hole, since, logically, the hole itself is "invisible."

You can see here a scheme of the gravitational force fields of stars like the sun (a), a neutron star (b), and a black hole (c). The gravitational pull of the black hole is much greater than the others!

2. At the end, a cosmic body is formed. It is so dense that its gravitational force greatly increases.

3. Gravity is so immense that it creates a "hole," which attracts everything.

4. Even light cannot escape, which is why it is called a black hole.

The Milky Way

The universe has diverse stars bunched in groups that form galaxies.

To which galaxy does our sun belong? Our galaxy is the Milky Way—a great accumulation of stars spread out in space in the shape of a flattened disk, of which we see only a small part. The Milky Way has the shape of a spiral and our sun is at the interior edge of one of its arms. Within the Milky Way, our sun is only a "very normal" star, since our galaxy contains approximately 100 billion stars.

The same way the planets of the solar system revolve around the sun, stars also revolve very fast around the center of the galaxy. This rotation has caused the flattening of the Milky Way into the shape of a disk.

Most of the known stars that form the Milky Way are inside the main disk of the galaxy and of its spiraling arms.

1. The Milky Way rotates at a speed of 558,000 miles (900,000 km) per hour, dragging the solar system in its movement.

What are shooting stars? Every year, during the second week of August, you can see in the sky a rain of shooting stars— dust fragments that have entered our atmosphere. When these fragments make contact with the air, they become very hot and volatile, shining in the night sky for fractions of seconds.

Do not think that we are at the center of the galaxy. The sun is located at the edge of the disk—30,000 light years away from the center of the Milky Way.

The Sagittarius region is in the central zone of the Milky Way.

3

2. It takes the Milky Way 200 million years to make one complete rotation.

3. The maximum diameter of the Milky Way is 100,000 light years.

Galaxies

Just as stars are grouped into galaxies, galaxies are grouped into swarms. When you look at the sky you can see faraway points of light that correspond to stars grouped in galaxies or in swarms of galaxies.

The two galaxies closest to us can be seen in the Southern Hemisphere. They are the Great Cloud of Magellan (160,000 light years away) and the Small Cloud of Magellan. The Andromeda galaxy is a spiral, rather like our own. It is "only" 2 million light years away. This means that the light we now see from this galaxy was sent more than 2 million years ago.

It is very difficult to imagine the size of the universe. The Milky Way, together with the Clouds of Magellan, the Andromeda galaxy, and approximately 30 other galaxies form a swarm called the Local Group. This is considered a rather small swarm, compared with others, such as the Virgin swarm, which includes a million galaxies!

It could happen that two galaxies meet in their travel through space. Despite the large number of stars that each of them contains, they never collide since they are billions of light years apart from each other.